Disclaimer

Please note that all definitions and illustrations expressed in this book are the views of the author. It does not represent the opinions of any entity whatsoever.

Methods favored as best practices in the past may quickly become obsolete as knowledge increases; hence readers must always rely on their own experience in analyzing and applying any information provided in this book.

The author, publisher, and anyone associated with writing this book shall not have any liability whatsoever for any losses, including losses for any omission, error, misinterpretation, or subsequent impact howsoever caused.

TABLE OF CONTENTS

Disclaimer

Please note that all definitions and illustrations expressed in this book are the views of the author. It does not represent the opinions of any entity whatsoever.

Methods favored as best practices in the past may quickly become obsolete as knowledge increases; hence readers must always rely on their own experience in analyzing and applying any information provided in this book.

The author, publisher, and anyone associated with writing this book shall not have any liability whatsoever for any losses, including losses for any omission, error, misinterpretation, or subsequent impact howsoever caused.

DEDICATION

Now all glory to God, who is able, through his mighty power at work within us, to accomplish infinitely more than we might ask or think.

Bible.

To Mmayen M. Pearls, my patient wife.

Many thanks to you for enduring through many months while authoring this book.

PREFACE

This third edition of Document Control Dictionary contains over 200 entries of simplified and intriguing definitions of common document control terminology, processes, and practices.

Whether you are a seasoned expert or a newcomer, you will find in this book the definitions of some of the technical jargon and terminology used in the document control profession daily.

You can reach out to me personally at olaris.guru@gmail.com. I hope you appreciate reading the book as much as I did writing it.

A

Advanced Copy

An advanced copy (also advance copy) of a document refers to a copy of that document sent or received to fast-track information sharing before its formal or official issuance.

In a project environment, for example, it is common practice for project teams to request and receive an advanced copy of a document from their counterparts for review or information while the responsible Document Controller prepares the transmittal package for formal issuance.

Annotations

Also Mark-up. Annotations are marks made on a document to draw the reader's attention to a specific section, to emphasize a point, or to quickly identify areas where changes or updates from the previous revision/version occurred.

Change tracking bars, revision triangles, circles, ovals, rectangles, clouds, and other symbols might be drawn around the modified part to make the annotations.

As a practice, when a newer revision is submitted for official release, Document Controllers should verify and confirm that all prior annotation marks have been deleted. Of course, any parts in the new revision where modifications are made should be annotated as such.

Approval

This is the action of authorizing or endorsing a document as suitable, adequate, and fit-for-purpose.

The recommended practice following the requirements of ISO 9001:2015 Quality management systems is for organizations to ensure appropriate review and approval for suitability and adequacy when creating and updating documented information.

Stamps or a set of signatures on a document are the most commonly used methods to indicate that a document has been reviewed and approved by the owners. Approval can be digital (using Document Control Software), electronic (e.g. the use of a scanned signature or stamp), or physical using wet signatures or samps.

Approval Cycle. See Review and Approval Cycle

Approver

An individual usually with corporate, technical, or contractual authority / responsible for approving a document. The Approver could be a General Manager, Engineering Manager, Project Manager, etc.

Archive

An archive is a collection of historical records or the repository (location) where records are preserved physically or electronically stored. The term "archive" when used as a verb means, "to keep the document in a designated repository."

It is important to note that archival management activities are more on the record, retention, and disposal management divide of information/document management than the document control end, which is responsible for the management and control of documents in their active life cycle stages.

As-Built Documents

In engineering projects, technical documents such as engineering drawings usually progress from 'Review' then to 'Approval' and finally to 'Construction' status. It is only the documents that are approved and attained 'Construction' status that is deemed suitable for constructing what needs to be constructed. However, the actual construction of the facility may not appear as-is in the approved design drawing due to several factors, such as unforeseen constraints in the field.

It is the final set of project documents showing the exact dimensions, geometry, and location of a structure, piece of equipment, or facility as it is built on the ground that we refer to as As-Built Documents.

Note:

- Changes to the approved design resulting from facility modification must be verified and correctly reflected on the final drawing and given the status "As-Built."
- Document Controllers must bear in mind that the As-Built documents would often be referenced by technical professionals for production, operations, and maintenance purposes. Managing As-Built documentation is thus an important aspect of safety.
- Engineers and document controllers should have a proper record tracking of field design changes and red mark-up drawings, which are the input document for the creation of As-Built documents.
- Where applicable, the contract document should have a section where the customer's

requirements for submission of As-Built documentation is specified.

Audit

PMBOK defines an audit

PMBOK defines an audit as *"a structured and independent review to determine whether project activities comply with the policies, procedures, and specifications of the project and performing organization."*

The International Standard, ISO 9000:2015, defines audit as a *"systematic, independent and documented process for obtaining objective evidence and evaluating it objectively to determine the extent to which the audit criteria are fulfilled."*

A process audit carried in document control will seek to inspect, verify, and ascertain that document control processes are functioning in line with applicable document control procedures, standards, or contractual requirements.

The three types of audits are first-party, second-party, and third-party. First-party audits are internal, while second and third-party audits are external audits. Organizations use first-party audits to (1) provide input for management review and (2) declare that they meet specified requirements - this is called a self-declaration.

When a client, for example, audits its supplier or contractor to ascertain compliance with requirements, it is called a second-party audit.

Third-party audits are external audits performed by registrars (certification bodies) or regulators to certify an organization to a particular standard.

Auditor

Person certified by a regulatory authority and appointed to conduct an audit.

Auditee

Person or organization being audited.

Author

Also Originator. A person responsible for writing document or modifying the content of an existing document. The author is responsible for the correctness of the documents' content.

B

Baseline Document

Any reference document that forms the basis against which performance or deviation of project component (schedule, cost, quality, scope of work, standard etc.) is measured with plan or expectation. Simply put, it is the original approved plan.

Examples of Baseline documents are FEED Specification, Production schedule, and scope of work. Note that the baseline document could be the original or a specific version.

Bookmarks

In this context, a bookmark is an address or mark that allows you to navigate, find or go quickly to specific points of a document rather than scrolling down through to that point.

Bridging Document

A document created to harmonize and align the practices and activities of two or more agencies participating in a risk-based operation.

For example, a contractor's HSE Procedure could be bridged with the client's HSE Procedure to produce a single document called the HSE Bridging Document. The rationale is to avoid conflict, foster best practices, and mutual understanding among the entities working on the same construction activity, for example, thereby reducing the risk level.

Brownfield Project
A project with existing facilities at the worksite. Examples include a project for the expansion, remodeling, or refurbishment of an existing exploration platform. All documents related to the existing facility are called Existing or Brownfield documents.

Bulk Upload
The action of auto-populating a repository or document control software with multiple documents and their associated metadata. The common tool used for performing bulk upload is a Comma Separated Values or Character Separated Values. *See CSV.*

C

CAD Drawings

Acronym for Computer-Aided Design. CAD are engineering drawings generated electronically by software.

Canceled Document, *See Obsolete Document*

Checker

Also Reviewer. A person who scrutinizes or verifies the technical content of a document. Usually, the direct supervisor of the document author.

Check-In / Check-out / Lock

The action or instance of retrieving a file from a repository, especially for the purpose of change, is referred to as check-out.

Check-in is just the opposite - putting a file into a repository. The concept of Check-In/Check-Out is common in Electronic Document Management Systems, EDMS, but it also applies to a manual filing system.

Unlike a manual filing system, most EDMS allows multiple users with the appropriate access credentials to check-out and modify the same document simultaneously from various terminals.

If a user wants to restrict others from accessing the document, he/she has to execute a separate action called Lock, which instructs the repository not to allow access or accept changes from others.

Note that certain EDMS locks a document when it is checked out.

Checklist

A checklist is a document used to carry out quality checks. Document Controllers routinely perform quality control checks on documentation, for example:

- To validate the correctness of traceability and identification information, including the document number, revision code, revision date, title, status code, page numbering, etc.
- To validate the quality, legibility, and correct use of templates, applicable font color, and size, logo, formatting, etc.
- To validate filename, review and approval of documents, etc.
- To validate the information mentioned in the document transmittal form against the actual document received.

In a project environment, it is a recommended practice to share document checklists with contractors and vendors so that the interfacing

Document Controllers can perform the same level of checks on document quality project-wide.

Comment Sheet

A Comment Sheet is a form for documenting the comment feedback received for a document submitted for review.

The use of a comment sheet in a typical project environment is as follows:

- The contractor submits a project document to the client for review,
- The reviewer on the client's side responds with review comments on a comment sheet which lets the contractor know whether to resubmit the document for review, approval, or to proceed to work with the document.

Note that:

- Some clients write their review comments directly on the document.
- The use of a comment sheet prompts and encourages document reviewers to provide their review comments in a structured manner, making it easier to consolidate.
- It is important to always keep the comment sheet for future reference and retrieval.

Commissioning

A project phase that is characterized by processes to confirm that a facility (for example, Gas Plant) has been designed, fabricated, installed, tested, and prepared for operation or production by the blueprint, design drawings, and specifications provided by the client.

Compliance. *See Conformity.*

Confidential Document

A document that contains sensitive or private information. A document classified as "confidential" implies that its unauthorized disclosure may damage the interests of an organization. As a result, Document Controllers typically rely on a controlled distribution matrix to help them through the process of appropriately distributing various types and categories of documents.

Other document security classification includes;
- Restricted – documents that may be freely shared within but not with third parties.
- Unrestricted – documents that may be shared without restrictions, and unlikely to result in any harm if disclosed to external parties.

Conformity

This is the condition of fulfilling a requirement. In its definition, the International Organization for Standardization book of vocabulary, ISO 9000:2015, notes the following:

- In English the word "conformance" is synonymous but deprecated.
- In French the word "compliance" is synonymous but deprecated.

Contract

A mutually binding agreement between a buyer and a seller that obliges the seller to provide the specified product, service, or result and obligates the buyer to make the payment for it.

Contractor

The party (person or organization), which carries out all or part of the management, design, engineering, procurement, construction or commissioning of a project, or the operation and maintenance of a facility under contractual terms and agreements.

Controlled and Uncontrolled Document

A document that is subjected to quality control actions such as document numbering, review, approval, registration, distribution, revision/version control, etc. The business history of controlled documents can be tracked easily because whenever such documents are created or modified, quality control actions will apply.

By default, all documents listed in a company or projects' Master Document Register, MDR, are controlled documents.

An uncontrolled document is not subject to quality control. Examples of uncontrolled documents include site photos, draft or working documents, personnel resumes, personal notes, etc.

The control of such a document is up to the individual or department that produces them. For example, if you update your resume, it does not matter whether you overwrite the previous version or save it with a new date in the filename before you send it out – with a controlled document, you cannot do this.

Correspondence

Any form of written communication in hardcopy or electronic format. Examples are letters, faxes, e-mails, transmittal notes, memos, minutes of meetings, Technical Queries, Request for Information, and Request for Inspection, etc.

Correspondences can be used for notification, seeking or giving clarifications and communicating decisions, etc.

Cover page

Also front cover, front page or title page. It is the first page of a document. The cover page of a document is useful for displaying both general information as well as specific identification and tracking details e.g. project title, company name, client and contractor logo, document number, revision, status, revision log, originator, a disclaimer on copyright, etc.

Document Controllers habitually check the cover page of a document for completeness and correctness of the information displayed.

Cryptographic Signature. See Digital Signature

CSV

An acronym for Comma Separated Values or Character Separated Values. It is a file format with a .csv extension for importing and exporting data or documents into and from database systems. As it is with many other spreadsheet files, a CSV file stores data in tabular arrangement with each row representing a record.

To save a spreadsheet file in .csv format, open the file from the spreadsheet program.

- Click File > Save As.
- Go to the "Save as type" drop down menu at the bottom of the Save As dialogue box

that appear,

- Select the CSV (Comma delimited) option,
- Click Save.

Note:

You may receive a system prompt that your file "may contain features that are not compatible with CSV." The reason is because CSV file format does not retain any formatting.

Cut-Off Date

A term used to specify a date limit. For example, a monthly progress report with cut-off date 30 April 2021 implies the report does not include progress information achieved beyond that 30 April 2021.

D

Data

Data refer to unorganized facts, items, or transactions that do not convey any specific meaning. Data items can be numbers, letters, figures, sounds, and images.

DDM. *See Document Distribution Matrix*

DDR. *See Master Document Register*

Decision Code

Also Comment Code or Review Code. These are codes used to denote a Reviewers' decision about the next line of action in a document life cycle. There are no universal decision codes - each organization or project will have their specifics.

See below examples of decision codes and their description:

Decision Codes	Description
1	The Document is approved. Affected work may proceed.
2	The Document is approved on condition. Affected work may proceed while the document is being modified and resubmitted.
3	The Document is reviewed with comments. Incorporate comments and resubmit. Work may not proceed.
4	The Document is rejected. Affected work must not proceed. Modify document / drawing and resubmit.

Deficiency list. See Punch List

Deliverable Documents

Documents agreed to be delivered by a work contractor to the customer (client) as a result of a project undertaken.

Demolition Drawings

Any existing drawing that shows the extent of the demolition work to be done.

Detailed Engineering Design, DED

An engineering project phase where the selected contractor(s) make necessary studies and develop comprehensive design drawings and specifications from Front End Engineering Drawing, FEED package.

Tender paperwork for subcontracting or procuring of equipment, as well as construction activities, are prepared based on DED deliverables. Document control activities are usually at a peak in this phase.

Deviation Request Form

A form used by a work contractor to formalize the process of requesting approval from the principal (client) to deviate from an initial technical specification or design requirement.

Digital signature

Also cryptographic signature. It is a type of electronic signature with security features. They are commonly used in Electronic Document Management Software or System, EDMS.

Document & Record

According to ISO 9000:2015 clause 3.8.5 a document is defined as, *"information and the medium on which it is contained"* whereas clause 3.8.10 defines a record as *"document stating results achieved or providing evidence of activities performed."*

In practice, the difference between both terms is usually subtle as almost all documents eventually become a record.

Below is a list of differences between a document and a record:

- Documents include records and non-records. Records are special documents containing evidence of past events.
- All documents are not records. All records are documents.
- Documents may be modified when necessary. Records are past events that cannot be modified.
- Examples of documents are work method statement, procedure, register, equipment

manual, permit to work, diagrams, and drawings, letters, minutes of meetings, etc. Examples of records are daily reports, letters, invoices, certificates, minutes of meetings, etc.

Document Control

Document Control is a proactive and methodological approach to managing documents throughout their life cycle.

Consepsys.com defines document control as "*a document management discipline whose purpose is to enforce controlled processes and practices for the creation, review, modification, issuance, distribution, and accessibility of documents.*"

Document Control Center, DCC

The office or basement of Document Controllers in an organization.

Document Control Coordinator

Also Lead Document Controller. This is a document control professional who leads a document control team on a project or in a department.

Document Control Instruction to Suppliers

A document control instructional guide issued to a contractor, equipment or service vendor. The purpose of the guide is to

- Guarantee accurate understating of the project's document control requirements, such as how to number documents, correct use of document templates, revisions, statuses etc.

- avoid repeating verbal communication on the correct document control criteria

- allow for consistency and uniformity in documentation between the buyer and supplier

Document Control Manager

Also Head of Document Control. A managerial position that oversees a company's document control system and staff.

Document Control Onboarding

A short learning process through which delegates or new employees get acquainted with the document control processes of an organization or project.

The topics in an onboarding session will vary from one organization or project to another. The typical topics in a Document Control Onboarding include but not limited to the following;

- Introduction to the organization or project document control rules, processes, tools and strategy
- Roles and Responsibility of users
- Applicable document templates, numbering system, revision codes, and statuses
- Document creation, review, and approval protocol
- Access to documentation and filing structure

Document Control Procedure, DCP

A document that sets out the rules and describes the requirements for the control of documents in a project, department, or entire organization.

Whether you are a seasoned expert or a newcomer, the DCP is one of the first documents you should read upon joining a new company to familiarize yourself with the applicable document control rules.

The procedure explains everything a user needs to know about the applicable document control process, including who does what, the sequence of operation, how to perform it, and anticipated output.

Examples of processes in a DCP include document numbering, review and approval of documents, revision control, management of superseded documents, distribution of documents, document transmittal, As-Built and Redlining, document handover, etc.

The Document Controller, as the custodian of the document management system, must comprehend and be able to interpret the provisions included therein.

Document Control Process

This is the set of interrelated steps and actions involved in controlling and managing documents throughout their lifecycle. Examples include, document creation, review, approval, distribution, archival, cancellation, handover, retention, and disposal, etc.

Document Controller, DC

An individual responsible for managing documents daily for a project, department, or entire organization. Depending on an organizations' size or the complexity of its processes, having a dedicated custodian who is accountable and in charge of document management is a recommended practice. Document Controllers in the engineering industry are sometimes addressed with informal titles such as:

- Corporate Document Controller (a DC working from any branch of the company home office and primarily manages corporate documentation)
- Site Document Controller (a DC working from a project site location)
- Engineering/Vendor Document Controller (a DC handling Engineering or Vendor documentation)

Document Creation and Modification Form

Also, Document Requisition (or Request) Form. A form used to standardize request such as

- Adding a new document to or deleting of an existing record from the document control master list
- Modifying the content, title, number of a document (on rare occasion)
- cancelling an existing document,

In a typical document requisition process, the requester fills out the appropriate document requisition form and returns a duly signed and approved copy to the Document Control Centre. This strategy is essential for controlling document change requests.

Document Deliverable Register. *See Master Deliverable Register*

Document Distribution

The act of making relevant versions of applicable documents available at points of use electronically via e-mail, an EDMS, or physically via hand delivery.

The distribution of documents is a sensitive activity in document management. It involves identifying key process owners and relevant persons/parties because an incorrectly circulated document can result in confusion, delayed action, disclosure of sensitive documents, loss of reputation and integrity of the organization, etc.

Document Distribution Matrix, DDM

DDM is a register that provides a visual guide for identifying the parties who should receive a particular document or category of documents.

The DDM will also contain what it expects the recipients to do.

For example, the distribution matrix could specify the distribution for all work method statements as follows:

- To the construction manager for review
- To the engineering manager, HSE manager, site manager, for information, and
- To the client for ultimate approval

In a project environment, the responsibility of

advising whom to include the document distribution matrix rests on the project manager.

Document Identification Number, DIN

DIN is a unique number or strings of characters assigned to one document and no other. DIN is an important document metadata (*information about the document*) that enables ease of its identification, filing and searching.

Document Lifecycle

The sequence of stages that a document goes through from its creation to its eventual archival or final destruction.

Document Management

Document management is how an organization stores, manages and tracks its documents.

A search query on the internet for "document management" usually returns with additional keywords such as "System", "Software", or "Solution". So ubiquitous is this conception that "document management" has inadvertently been dubbed "software to manage documents".

Perhaps this is due to the proliferation of document management software and the associated market competition.

Document Numbering Procedure

A document that specifies a company's document numbering conventions. It instructs the user on how to number the organization's documented information. The procedure will include the lists of codes for document types, revisions, statuses, plants, and their location, etc. act.

Document Requisition (or Request) Form. *See Document Creation and Modification Form*

Document Status and Status Codes

Document status is the milestone or progress level of a document in its developmental life cycle. There are no universal document statuses: however, to maintain some decorum, it makes sense to adopt patterns of codes typically used your industry.

Examples of common document statuses are shown below, along with their codes in parenthesis:

- Approved for Construction (AFC) / Approved for Fabrication (AFF) - Milestone indicating that the document has been reviewed and approved for use or construction activities.
- Approved for Design (AFD) - Milestone used to indicate that the document has been

reviewed and approved for design development, and procurement.

- Issued for Construction (IFC) – Milestone used to indicate when a document/drawing is formally distributed for construction approval.
- Issued for Information (IFI) – Status indicating that the document is for information only.
- Issued for Review (IFR) – Milestone used to indicate a document review.
- Issued for Approval (IFA) – Milestone used to indicate when a document is formally distributed for approval.
- Approved for Tender, Bidding (AFT, AFB) – Milestone used to indicate that the document is approved by the authorized person for the tendering process.
- Issued for Purchase Approval (IFP) - Milestone used to indicate when a document is formally distributed for purchase approval.
- Approved For Purchase (AFP) – Milestone used to indicate that the document is approved by the authorized person for the purchasing process.
- Issued For Tender Approval (IFT) - Milestone used to indicate when a

document is formally distributed for tender approval.

- Issued for Design (IFD) – Milestone used to indicate when a document is formally distributed for design approval.
- As-Built (ASB) – Milestone used to indicate that the content of the document reflects the exact geometry and dimensions of a facility or equipment as built on the ground.
- Canceled (CAN) – Status indicating that the document is canceled and no longer valid.
- Draft (DFT) - A document in work-in-progress stage.

Document Title
The name assigned to the document.

Document Workflow
The administrative processes a document goes through in its lifecycle.

Documentation
We understand from Note 2 of ISO 9000:2015, clause 3.8.5, that a collection of documents such as specifications and records, is commonly referred to as "documentation."

Documented Information

ISO 9000:2015 clause 3.8.2 defines Documented Information as *"information required to be controlled and maintained by an organization and the medium on which it is contained."*

Draft

A Draft is a document in working stage suitable for internal use only.

E

EDMS

An acronym for Electronic Document Management System (Solution or Software). It is a generic term for any computer application used to store and manage electronic records, data, and documents.

Examples of popular EDMS are SharePoint, Assai, Aconex, Laserfiche, Alfresco, Docuware, Documentum, etc.

Due to the high cost of implementing EDMS, most organizations usually have an Excel spreadsheet application to manually keep track of document life cycle, and a secured shared drive to store documents. In most cases, an EDMS does both.

Important Note:

Top management frequently commits EDMS implementation projects to the ICT Experts without actively engaging Document Controllers or those directly involved in the day-to-day management of the organization's documents. End-users would frequently quit such a system because they will work hard to get it to accept standard document control practices that were not addressed during the system requirement gathering/analysis.

When choosing the best EDMS to purchase, it is best to consult all essential stakeholders, especially the document controllers.

Electronic documents

Any media information that is created, transmitted, delivered, received, or stored electronically.

Electronic signature

Marks, text, symbols, etc. that represent acknowledgment of an electronic message, transaction, or document. For example, a scanned image of a handwritten signature or a typed name at the end of an email.

Email

Email is a messaging service that allows you to send and receive asynchronous messages. The typical workday of a Document Controller's consists of reading and reacting to internal and external emails about documentation issues. The following is a collection of best practices and useful guide when using email applications:

- Read and understand the company email Etiquettes.
- Think whether a telephone call or physical contact will be safer or more efficient rather than sending an email.
- The subject of an email should clearly state the project code (where applicable) and be self-explicatory. This is also important for traceability.
- Blank subject should be completely avoided.
- Avoid creating "marathon" emails with the same subject on several different topics. Write a new message when a different topic is being addressed.
- Except otherwise necessary, an e-mail should be addressed to a single recipient, while only personnel concerned should be in copy (cc).
- Avoid including clients, suppliers, or

external parties in cc for e-mails addressed to colleagues, especially when requesting action of any kind.

- Do not leave the recipient guessing what to do. State your reason for sending an email (e.g. for review, attention, information, approval, record, etc.).
- For large attachments use servers or document exchange tools if available.
- Use company approved E-mail disclaimer
- Proper personal identification should be present in mail correspondence. An electronic signature is an appropriate tool for that purpose.

Sample E-mail signature:
> *Person's name*
> *Designation*
> *Office address*
> *Phone Numbers*
> *Website Address*

EPC

An acronym for Engineering Procurement and Construction. EPC firms undertake activities involving engineering, procurement, and construction of facilities such as refineries, power plants, mineral processing & mining, etc.

External Document

Documents that you receive from an external organization. For example, a Purchase Order or Product Specification from client.

F

Fabrication, Construction, and Assembly

A phase of a project's execution that involves the creation and assembly of pieces of equipment, pipes, and other systems.

Field Design Change, FDC, Form

A form for proposing a design change to an engineering document that has previously received approval for construction. Request for field design changes usually arises during construction due to site constraints or conflicting conditions.

File

A collection of document or folder for holding data, document, or information together.

Document Controllers handle various types and forms of files including: data files, text files, computer program files, directory files, physical and electronic documents, photographs, microfilms, audio recordings, videotapes, CDs and DVDs, etc.

Filename

The name of an electronic document on a hard drive. We can also describe it as the identification name given to a file (document) when it is saved on a computer hard disk.

Final Document Handover

The transfer of project information assets (document and data) from a work contractor to the owner or customer.

It is often difficult to address the requirements for final document handover at the start of a project. For example, "In what format should the information be submitted?" "How many copies are to be submitted?" "How should it be packaged?" "What is the submission sequence and the place of delivery?" These questions are frequently left unanswered until the handover period.

For these reasons, it is usual to see both the contractor and customer rushing to complete the handover process because, on the one hand, the customer is anxious to acquire the long-awaited plant/equipment and, on the other, the work contractor is anxious to collect the handover milestone payment.

All these make the handover documentation process a significant experience for Document

Controllers. Regrettably, employers usually downsize their workforce including Document Controllers as the project nears completion for obvious reasons.

Important Notes:

- Where the handover requirements are not expressly specified in the contract, a dedicated meeting between client and contractor handover team should be convened to discuss the gray areas of the project document handover requirements.
- The meeting's deliberations should be recorded in the meeting's minutes, which should be verified by the attendees for accuracy before being signed and circulated.
- Work Contractor should develop and submit a handover management plan containing the handover deliverable index.
- A final handover transmittal note should be prepared to accompany the handover dossier/package. The transmittal note should also be duly signed (acknowledged) by the receiver.

Focal Person

During an inter-discipline review process, a Focal Person is a chosen representative of a team, such as an engineer, who organizes the document review operations. All inputs (review comments) obtained from the team or ancillary reviewers are gathered and consolidated by the focus person into one final set.

Form

A document with blank spaces for data or information to be filled in. Examples of forms used in document control are the Transmittal form, Document Requisition Form, etc.

Freeze

The action of setting a register or schedule in a fixed state at a point in time. For example, a projects' document deliverable registration may be frozen at a certain point in a project's life cycle so that additional deliverables from the freeze date would not impact the documentation progress already attained.

Front End Engineering Design (FEED)

A phase of engineering project development in which the functional properties of system components are examined, and numerous studies are conducted to identify technical concerns and estimate preliminary investment costs.

This project phase offers the most opportunity for resource optimization and selecting the best solutions and techniques for the DED (Detailed Engineering Design).

Front Page. *See Cover Page*.

Greenfield Project
A project where there are no pre-existing facilities.

H

Head of Document Control. *See Document Control Manager*

Header and Footer
The header is the top margin of each page of a document, while the footer is the bottom margin of each page of a document. These sections of a document hold key document information like title, revision code, page numbers, etc.

Hold Point
Hold point is a critical action or verification point requiring the approval of a designated authority before an activity can progress to the next stage.

Hypertext transfer protocol (HTTP)
A protocol commonly used to access resources on the Internet.

I

IDC. *See Inter-Discipline-Check*

Information

Organized data that has meaning and value to the recipient.

Information management

ARMA International defines Information management as the practice of ensuring a consistent flow of organizational information through a defined lifecycle that starts with its conception or capture through to its archival or disposition.

Inspection Call. *See Request for Inspection*

Inter-Discipline-Check, IDC

Also Squad Check. Document review performed across multiple disciplines or organizations.

Internal Document

Any document generated internally by an organization.

International Organizations for Standardization, ISO

ISO is an independent and non-governmental network of national standard bodies poised with the responsibility of formulating a globally acceptable standard requirement for organizations.

It is probably the most widely used global standard that specifies the requirements of document control.

ISO framework is developed to address the global challenge of consistently meeting customer requirements/satisfaction in the ever-changing business environment. For example, ISO 14000 is the family of environmental management standards formulated to provide a guide and framework for organizations intending to improve their Environmental management performance whereas, ISO 9000 deals with the Quality Management Systems of an organization.

ISO QUICK FACTS:

- Founded on February 23, 1947.
- Headquartered in Geneva, Switzerland.

- ISO is not an abbreviation or acronym. It is a Greek word meaning equal.
- It is a non-governmental organization but acts as a consortium with strong links to governments.
- Purpose: International Standardization
- Individuals or companies cannot become ISO members.
- ISO has three membership categories (Member body, Correspondent members, and Subscriber members)
- There is only one member per country representing the foremost body of standard in their countries.
- There are, as of January 2018, 168 member countries.
- There are, as of January 2018, 162 national membership.
- Developing new standards usually takes about three (3) years interval.
- ISO standards are drafted by members in technical committees when there is a request from industry or other stakeholders such as consumer groups to meet a market concern.

- The draft is subjected to a consensus voting to become an ISO standard. Where agreement could not be reached, the draft may be further modified and voted again.
- ISO is not involved in certification and does not issue certificates.
- External certification bodies issues certificates and not ISO.
- According to ISO official website, https://www.iso.org/certification.html, when labeling a product or system as certified to an ISO standard, do not say "ISO certified" or "ISO certification." Instead, say "ISO 9001:2015 certified" or "ISO 9001:2015 certification" (for example)

Internet
The vast network of computer systems that enables worldwide connectivity among users and computers.

Inter-Office Memo. *See Memorandum*

Intranet
An internal or private network that cannot be accessed by anyone outside that network.

Invitation to Tender/ Bid. *See Request for Quotation*

ISO. *See International Organizations for Standardization*

Issue Code

Also, submission code or Purpose of Issue. Code used in a transmittal note to let the recipient know why he or she is receiving the documents contained in the transmittal package. The code may indicate that the document being sent is for information, review, approval, action or use, etc.

ITT. *See Request for Quotation*

K

Kickoff Meeting, KOM

Following the award of a contract, the KOM is the first official meeting of important stakeholders, including document controllers. Clients and contractors, for example, can use KOM to discuss and agree on the project execution strategy.

KPI

An acronym for Key Performance Indicator. KPI provides an excellent mechanism for measuring the degree to which a system or process meets set objectives. KPIs are not generic but usually customized to a project or organization's objectives.

KPIs could be formulated based on:

- **Efficiency**; to monitor or gauge the efficiency and performance of a process
- **Quality;** to measure the degree to which customer expectations and quality requirements are meet
- **Safety**; to measure fatalities and LTI (lost time injuries)
- **Time**; to determine the duration of a process
- **Cost**: to measure cost implications

Examples of KPIs set for Document Control may include:

- The average time between the arrival of a transmittal/document and its distribution to stakeholders
- Percentage document rejected due to bad quality
- Percentage of recorded non-conformity on

documentation
- Average time to retrieve a document
- Number of cases of missing documents
- Number of Document Controllers that have vocational training Advisory/Best Practice Tips

L

Lead Document Controller. *See Document Control Coordinator*

Liquidated Damages

Claims or penalties levied on an organization for breach, such as late or delayed completion of a project.

Live Document

A document whose content changes frequently and is consequently updated (evergreen) throughout its life cycle. A good example is a project's master document register, MDR.

M

Management of Change Procedure

A procedure through which implementation of changes or decisions that may negatively impact equipment, people, environment, quality, cost, schedule, or scope of work are adequately reviewed, authorized, or rejected.

Manufacturer's Record Book, MRB Vs Vendor Record Book, VRB

Also, Manufacturer's Data Book and Vendor Data Book. These phrases are often used interchangeably, however, there is a subtle distinction to be made. When a customer procures a product (e.g., equipment, instrument) in the Oil and Gas business, the Vendor or OEM often submits a dossier of documentation detailing the product to the owner (client). Some vendors package the dossier and transmit it as an MRB or VRB. So, what are the distinctions?

MRB	VRB
Document package containing all applicable certificates	Document package containing all applicable technical

and other quality control documents for the product.	documents approved for the design of the product.
Evidence that the product is certified by the governing authorities and confirmed ok.	Evidence that the product is designed based on the technical documents as approved.
Examples of documents that make up the MRB are Certificate of Conformity, Certificate of Origin, Certificate of Conformity, Mill Certificates, quality plan, Test and Inspection Reports, etc.	Examples of documents that make up the VRB are General arrangement drawing, specifications, datasheet, nameplate drawing, etc.

Mark-ups. *See Annotations*

Master Document Register, MDR

In general, MDR is the list of documents an organization or project deems necessary, suitable, and adequate for its activities. In project settings, "Master Deliverable Register" is more appropriate. It is the list or register identifying the minimum documents a contractor is expected to generate to carry out project work and also deliver to the client after the project completion. Variants of MDR include Document Deliverable Register, DDR, Vendor Document Register, VDR, Supplier Document Register, SDR, etc.

Mechanical completion

A phase in an engineering project where equipment and systems (piping, electrical, mechanical, etc.) are checked to make sure everything is installed as per requirements.

Memorandum

Also Inter-Office Memo. A document used for disseminating internal communication within an organization.

Meta-data

Information or attribute of a document. Examples of metadata include document type, size, creation date, number, title, discipline, classification, revision, and version, etc.

Method Statement. *See Work Instruction*

Milestone

A significant stage or point reached in the life of a project, document, or activity.

Minutes of Meetings, MOM

The instant written record of a meeting or hearing. MOM typically describes the events and deliberations at the meeting.

It is a good practice to sign the final copy of the MOM by a representative of each party involved and distribute the same to all participants.

N

Native Files

Any file generated from a particular software or program with a proprietary format that may not be editable or recognized by other programs. For example, when the Microsoft Word application saves a file in .doc or .docx file formats, we say it is native to the Microsoft Word application.

In other words, a native file on your computer without the corresponding application program may be useless to you.

Non-Compliance. *See Compliance*

O

OCR
Acronym for Optical character recognition. Technology that converts images of typed, handwritten or printed text into machine-readable text.

Obsolete Documents
A document could be said to be obsolete for any of the below reasons:

- It is no longer correct,
- It has been superseded (replaced) by a newer revision,
- The project or product it pertains to has been discontinued, or
- It is declared obsolete by an authorized person for any other reason.

To put it another way, an "obsolete document" is one that has been canceled, superseded, annulled, and voided.

Management of obsolete documents is important in document control because if they are utilized inadvertently (mistakenly), they can have serious financial and safety consequences. As a result, it is critical to include how obsolete documents will be managed in the document control guiding procedure. For instance,

- A document that has been superseded must be stamped with a red stamp that reads "OBSOLETE" OR "SUPERSEDED".
- All superseded documents must be transferred to a separate folder labeled "obsolete documents."
- Include a disclaimer that, "end-users are responsible for checking documents in their possession with the revision in the document control center."

OEM

Acronym for Original Equipment Manufacturer. A company that produces equipment.

Offline Document Review

Offline Document Review is a document review conducted without passing through the document control process.

In as much as offline review is encouraged to gain traction, completely ignoring document control processes, for example, in the review and approval of documents, could eventually result in delay, confusion, mix-up, and other grave documentation bottlenecks.

Originator. *See Author*

Outstanding Document Report

A report that lists listing the documents whose review, approval, or submission is pending but not necessarily in delay as in an overdue report.

Overdue Document Report

A report that lists documents that have been delayed in review, approval, or submission in comparison to scheduled/planned dates or contractual deadlines.

Owner/Client/Principal

These terms are used interchangeably in a project to denote the party, which initiates the project and eventually pays for its execution. The Owner specifies the technical requirements of a project, reviews, and approves design documents received from the responsible work contractor, or engages an agent or consultant to act on its behalf.

P

PDF

Acronym for Portable Document Format. It is a file format used to present and exchange documents reliably, independent of software, hardware, or operating system.

It was invented in the year 1991 by Adobe and cofounder Dr. John Warnock but is now an open standard maintained by the International Organization for Standardization (ISO).

PDFs can contain links and buttons, form fields, audio, video, business logic and it is the most trusted format used by businesses around the world.

Plot Plan

Also site plan. Engineering scale drawing showing the buildings, utility, equipment layout, position of roads, etc., of an existing or proposed project site.

Pre-Commissioning

Project phase that comes after mechanical completion. Pre-commissioning activities include cleaning, flushing, drying, testing (e.g. leak test, hydro-testing) of unit equipment and operating systems such as piping systems. It paves the way for Commissioning.

Sometimes pre-commissioning activities are performed in mechanical completion depending on the contract conditions or the requirement of the project. Extensive use of check sheets helps to guide the commissioning process.

Procedure

A specified way to carry out an activity or a process. *Definition from ISO 9001:2015 Quality management systems - Fundamentals and vocabulary.*

Process

A set of interrelated or interacting activities that use inputs to deliver an intended result. *Definition from ISO 9001:2015 Quality management systems - Fundamentals and vocabulary.*

Process Flow Diagram

An an engineering drawing showing the major equipment, the direction of process (liquid, gas) flow, and the basic process controls within a facility limit.

Project

PMBOK describes a project as *"a temporary endeavor undertaken to create a unique product, service, or result"*.

ISO 900:2015 Quality management systems defines it as a *"unique process consisting of a set of coordinated and controlled activities with start and finish dates, undertaken to achieve an objective conforming to specific requirements including the constraints of time, cost and resources"*

Project Schedule

A document showing the plan for the preparation, execution, and completion of a project, as well as a list of activities to be completed within a given time frame.

Punch List

Also Deficiency list. A list of items marked as unfinished, outstanding, or malfunctioning during commissioning activity or after a project's completion.

Purchase Order

A Purchase Order, PO, (or Service Order) is a commercial document with underlying contract terms issued by a buyer to a seller to authorize an offer to procure products or services.

It is a recommended practice to include a Supplier or Vendor Document Requirement Listing in the PO package for products or services that requires documentation.

Purpose of Issue. *See Issue Code*

Q

Quality

The degree to which a set of inherent characteristics fulfills requirements". *Definition from ISO 9001:2015 Quality management systems - Fundamentals and vocabulary.*

Quality management system (QMS)

The set of interrelated quality elements (policies, processes, and procedures) with which an organization can meet customers' and other applicable requirements consistently.

R

Record. *See Document*

Record Management

ARMA International defines records management as *"the professional field dedicated to the information that rises to the level of importance that requires ongoing maintenance, whether it be for evidentiary or specific business purposes."*

Redlining

The act of using colored pens (usually red color) to capture comments and changes to design drawings.

Repository. *See Archive*

Request for Inspection

Also Inspection Call. A correspondence document used to formalize the process of inviting a party such as a client, to witness or examine a facility, material, or equipment.

Request for Quotation

Other variants include, Request for Proposal and Invitation to Tender. These are procurement document package used to solicit bids from vendors or contractors to supply goods or provide services.

In practice, the differences between these terms are often subtle; however, a clearer understanding of the differences will enable the responsible procurement team to prepare the right contract statement and consequently facilitate receiving the correct response from bidders.

Request for Quotation, RFQ (also Request for Quote) is the simplest method of bid solicitation used for low-priced valued products and services.

The concept of RFQ is geared towards obtaining and using the best price offer criteria for the selection of vendors/suppliers. In an RFQ, the product and/or service to be procured are adequately specified and therefore easily measurable and quantifiable without ambiguity. In RFQ, suggestions from bidders for alternative products or services are usually not considered. Vendors respond to an RFQ with a quotation document having cost and description/list of exact service to be rendered or product to be procured.

The purchaser can compare prices amongst the various quotation received from the bidding vendor/suppliers with ease due to the clear and rigid specification of RFQ. An example of the usage of RFQ is in contract to supply standard off-the-shelf items.

Request for Proposal, RFP, is a more complex solicitation method than RFQ. A solicitor seeking a solution or a better way to achieve a result will use an RFQ, preferably.

The best criterion for the selection of vendors in RFP is the vendor's proposed technical approach.

In RFP, the solicitor knows the overall scope of the job but usually does not understand the details or have the requisite human or time resources to do the job.

The solicitor, therefore, sought competent vendors who understand the request, possess the required technical capability, and the best approach/solution to the need. Price is not of primary concern here but a technical solution.

Vendors respond to an RFP by submitting a proposal.

It is usual for vendors to propose alternative solutions for the job requested in an RFP. The solicitor will then decide and select the vendor based on the technical approach and then cost. Due to these alternatives, the cost is not easily comparable in an RFP.

Invitation to Tender, ITT (also Invitation to Bid, Request for Tender Notice) is somewhere between RFQ and RFP. The selection of vendors is based on cost and technical skills.

Vendors respond to an ITT with a tender document. The clarity of the specification in an ITT makes prices among various tenders easily comparable. Since the purchasers' specifications/requirements are specific and quantifiable, alternatives are not usually considered in an ITT.

Retention and Disposal Schedule

Organizations usually follow a retention and disposal schedule as part of their obligation to retain records for a specified time frame and also to apply appropriate means of disposal at the end of the retention period.

What determines the retention and disposal schedule of records include contractual requirements in the case of a project, the value of the record, legal and statutory requirements, best practice, etc.

The retention period could be for a certain

number of years or permanent. At the expiration of a time-bound retention period, the concerned record must be disposed of properly and not carelessly.

Common methods of record and document disposal are shredding or transfer to a permanent archive.

Recommended practices for retention and disposal schedule,

- Develop a realistic Retention Plan/Schedule.
- Departmental heads should check and review the schedule periodically.
- Contract documents should clearly state the retention period for project documentation. Upon expiration of the retention period, documented information (electronic and hardcopy), should be disposed of in an appropriate manner, e.g. by shredding.
- For convenience, records may be retained in certain instances longer than the minimum retention period.
- Document retention & disposal procedure should be written to govern what should be retained, where retained documents will be stored, for how long, how should they be transferred, and to whom?

Retrieval

The process of getting a document from its repository.

Review

The act of scrutinizing or analyzing a document for correctness

Review and Approval Cycle

The phase in the lifecycle of a document where the document goes through review and approval before its official use. The activities involved in this phase include document distribution for review, incorporating comments from reviewers, 'up-revving' the document, authorization (approval), distribution to the place of use, and registration of each activity in the document control log.

Reviewer. *See Checker*

Revision

Any official edition or publication of a document.

Revision codes or index

Codes assigned to each formal edition of a document to differentiate each revision. Revision codes can be numeric, alphabetic, alphanumeric, date-based, etc.

Examples of revision codes 1.0, 2.0, A, B, R01, Z01,

C01, 00, 01, D01, etc.

Revision Control

Also Version Control. Revision Control is a system put in place to correctly identify and manage a document's numerous versions. Thus, every time a document is updated officially, a new revision must emerge with a new revision index assigned.

As a result of these measures, users are less likely to work with outdated documents. The revision control of an organization's documented information is one of the controls required by ISO 9001:2015.

Revision History Table/Log

A tabular record within a document that keeps track of the document's revisions.

The table may include the record of the existing revision codes, the corresponding revision date, document status, and sometimes a summary description of modification made.

Revision System

a coding scheme that all revisions (official editions) of a controlled document must follow religiously as they undergo updates or progresses through their lifecycles. For example, a company using numerical revision codes may formulate a revision system as follow:

- 1st revision of any controlled document shall be coded Rev01
- 2nd revision = Rev02
- 3rd revision = Rev03
- 4th and subsequent revisions = Rev04, Rev05, Rev06... and so on.

Rev-up

Rev-up (or up-rev) is a document control jargon coined perhaps from the phrase 'Up the Revision.' It means progressing a document from its current revision to the next appropriate revision. For example, if a document currently in revision 02 is updated, it will be officially published in revision 03 following the applicable revision system.

S

Scope of Work, SoW

A statement that outlines the extent of work undertaken or to be done to deliver a projects' products, services, or results.

SDRL. *See Supplier Document Requirement List*

_____

SDS. *See Supplier Document Schedule*

Senior Document Controller

A more experienced Document Controller.

Service Order. *See Purchase Order*

Shared-Drive

Shared-Drive is a networked computer folder where people on the network and with the access privilege could access from their workstation.

In the absence of an EDMS, the importance of a project shared drive cannot be underestimated – it provides a central point that enables the project team to have access to real-time updates of documents.

To avoid the loss of electronically stored documents due to server failure, organizations using a server-based folder must implement a good backup strategy or contingency plan. It is a big business frustration to experience an unrecoverable server failure.

Shop Drawings

Drawings developed from approved engineering drawings with additional details for the actual fabrication of equipment.

Typically, a shop drawing will show more construction details than the engineering drawings do.

In summary, shop drawings provide extra information for construction in the manufacturer's workshop, whereas engineering drawings describe the proposed structure.

Squad Check. *See Inter-Discipline-Check*

Stamp

An office tool used to place identification or authorization mark, symbol, signature, etc. on a document. A document stamped as "SUPERSEDED" for example, indicates that that document has a more updated version or revision.

Standard Operating Procedure (SOP)

Documents developed within the Quality Management System of an organization to provide direction and guidelines to be followed routinely for performance of designated operations in designated situations

Examples of SOPs include Document System and Structure Management, Vendor Management, Process Framework, etc.

The SOPs in an organization's QMS are narrowed down into instructional documents for completing each major activity. For example, a project document control procedure.

Status Codes. *See Document Status*

Sub-Contractor

Organization or person hired to perform a part or all the work scope for which a main or prime contractor has committed itself under contractual terms and conditions.

Submission Code. *See Issue Code*

Superseded. *See Obsolete Document and Version Control*

Supplier Document Register. *See Master Deliverable Register*

Supplier Document Requirement List, SDRL

Also Vendor Document Requirement List VDRL A is a list of documentation requirements generated by a purchaser for a contract or purchase order. The SDRL will be used by the responsible Supplier for the development of a Supplier Document Register/Schedule.

It is a recommended practice to include a VDRL in an Invitation to Tender package as well as the final Purchase Order package.

Supplier Document Schedule, SDS

SDS is a supplier's document deliverable list showing the scheduled submission dates of each document listed therein.

T

Technical Bid Evaluation

A report covering the technical information obtained from inquiry and evaluation of proposals/tenders received from selected bidders.

Technical Query Form

A document correspondence used to formalize the request for technical information or clarification during the design phase of an engineering project.

Template

A pre-formatted document that serves as a starting point for creating a new document or an example of how a completed document should look like.

Using the correct document template in a project or corporate setting is a major issue to deal with in document control. As a result, Document Controllers must ensure that approved templates are readily available to users from the start. They are also there to maintain and insist on the use of the appropriate and approved document templates.

Title Block

A section of a document or a drawing that is dedicated to displaying important document traceability and/or identification information. Examples of information that goes into the title block are the document title, number, type, originating company/department, author, project name, plant, plant location, revision, status, revision date, etc.

Traceability

The extent to which a document's history or what transpired throughout its lifecycle can be tracked. For example, who reviewed the document, when it was last reviewed, what changed between revisions, and what is the current revision, etc.

Regardless of the high amount of document inflow and outflow daily, an organization that implements document control will be able to trace the history of every controlled document.

Transmittal Note

Also Transmittal Cover, Transmittal Form, or Transmittal Letter. A transmittal is a form or receipt that accompanies documents sent officially from one party (department, organization, or individual) to another.

The transmittal form can be compared to a courier waybill. When a courier package is delivered, the recipient the waybill to acknowledge receipt of the delivery.

In the same vein, acknowledging transmittal is a recommended practice. The acknowledgment is not an endorsement or approval of the documents listed in the transmittal, but rather a confirmation of receipt of the document.

Note: Transmittals you sent out are called outgoing transmittals, while transmittals you receive are called incoming transmittals.

Transmittal Package

A transmittal package is simply a transmittal note together with the documents listed in the transmittal note. The package is prepared by a Document Controller in one organization and sent to the document control center of another - the receiving organization. It is usually delivered electronically (e.g. as an email, or downloaded via FTP site or EDMS) in a zipped folder. Where applicable, it can also be distributed in print format.

Transmittal Register

A register that records the information included in incoming and outgoing transmittals. The transmittal reference number, date of issuance or reception, name/address of the originating and receiving organizations, identification number of the documents transmitted, titles, modifications, statuses, and so on are all examples of information found in the transmittal record.

Turn-Key Project

A turn-key project is one in which a contractor commits to designing, procuring, building, installing, and finishing a facility before handing it over to the owner once it is operational or ready for use.

When the project is finished and delivered by the work contractor, the customer just "turns a key," as it were, to start it in motion.

The engineering, procurement, and construction of refineries, power plants, mineral processing and mining, and oil and gas plants are all examples of turn-key projects.

U

Uncontrolled Document. *See Controlled Document*

Up-Rev. *See Rev-up.*

V

Variation Request Form

A document that is used to standardize requests for changes to a contract's pricing due to change in the scope of work.

VDR. *See Master Deliverable Register*

VDRL. *See Supplier Document Requirement List*

Vendor

Any organization that supplies material or equipment to a buyer.

Vendor Document Register, *See Master Deliverable Register*

Vendor Record Data Book. *See Manufacturer's Record Book*

Version

Any of the editions of a document resulting from modification. There may be various versions of a document throughout its existence, but only a few revisions - official publication or edition.

Users are responsible for managing document

versions in their possession, whereas Document Controllers maintain the formal publications known as revisions.

Version also refers to a document's form such as paper or electronic versions.

Version control. *See Revision Control*

Vital Record

A vital record is a document that is critical to the function, operation, and continuity of an organization, as well as its recovery in the event of a disaster.

Wet Signature

A physical signature on a document. The adjective "wet" comes from the fact that ink takes time to dry.

Work Breakdown Structure, WBS

A discrete outline or breakdown of project work into manageable units called work packages.

Work Completion Certificate, WCC

A document certifying that a task e.g. a project work has been finished following the contract's terms, conditions, and specifications.

Work Instruction

Also Method Statement or Work Method Statement. A document that that describes in detail, the steps and sequence of instructions on how to complete a specific task or activity.

Work Package

A set of activities or tasks that may be estimated and managed as a unique workload. From the standpoint of planning, it might alternatively be regarded as a division of the job scope into smaller groups of activities.

Each group or work pack comprises deliverable documents, the overall progress of which defines the completion of the work package in question.

Workflow. *See Document Workflow*

Working document. *See Draft*

INDEX